THE PARTHENON
IN
NASHVILLE

From a personal viewpoint

By

Wilbur F. Creighton

ATHENA PARTHENOS
completed by sculptor
Alan LeQuire
in 1990

ATHENA PARTHENOS
A Brief Nashville History

Created by Nashville sculptor Alan LeQuire over an eight-year period, Athena Parthenos is the only full-scale recreation of the statue of the Greek goddess Athena, which once stood in the Parthenon in Athens, Greece. LeQuire worked with an international team of scholars to ensure that this work accurately represents the ancient original, which has been lost for centuries. Standing 42 feet high, Nashville's Athena Parthenos is the tallest indoor sculpture in the Western World. The final assembly of its sculpted parts in the Nashville Parthenon completes the world's only exact-size replica of one of history's most renowned buildings.

Each plume of the helmet is supported by a mythological beast: a sphynx in the center and a pegasus (winged horse) on either side.

The helmet cheek pieces are folded up as sign of peace. In battle they would be folded down to protect the ears and cheeks. A griffin is carved on each: griffins guard the four corners of the Parthenon.

In Athena's right hand rests a six-foot tall statue of Nike, the goddess of victory, who holds a wreath with which she is about to crown Athena. This is probably a reference to the recent victory Athens had won over the Persians.

The soles of Athena's sandals are carved with scenes from the battle of the Lapiths and the Centaurs, a story which is also represented in the metopes of the Doric frieze that encircles the outside of the Parthenon.

Across the front of the base supporting Athena is a frieze of 21 figures which represents the birth of Pandora (the first woman in Greek mythology), who was sculpted by Hephaistos, one of the sons of Zeus. In order, from left to right, the figures are: Helios, Hermes, Hera, Zeus, Nike, Dionysos, the three Horai, Pandora, Hephaistos, Athena, Poseidon, Artemis, Apollo, Ares, Demeter, Hestia, Eros, Aphrodite, Selene.

Athena's breastplate is called the aegis. It was made from a magic goatskin which made the wearer invulnerable and was given to Athena by Zeus, her father.

In the center of the breastplate is the head of Medusa, the gorgon who has snakes for hair. Athena gave Perseus the magic shield which he used like a mirror to cut off Medusa's head without being turned to stone. He gave the head to Athena in appreciation. Medusa's head also appears in the center of the shield.

Eleven snakes appear in Athena's breastplate, belt and bracelet. The snake is symbolic of life and renewal, since the snake sheds his skin every year.

The large snake between Athena and her shield is probably Ericthonios, a legendary king of Athens. He represents the people of Athens who are protected by Athena.

The shield is elaborately carved with scenes of the battle between the Greeks and the Amazons. The wall of the Acropolis is visible, as is the facade of the Parthenon in the background at the top.

A Brief Ancient History

Considered to be the greatest achievement of Phidias, the pre-eminent sculptor of Ancient Greece, the original Athena Parthenos was an excellent example of the high degree of artistic sophistication achieved by the ancient masters. Crafted of ivory and gold over a wooden frame, the ancient Athena Parthenos epitomized the golden age of Athens under the rule of Pericles-- when freedom of thought, art and statesmanship held high the meaning of life. The gold and ivory statue was lost in the Fifth Century, approximately 900 years after its creation.

Dedicated to

WILBUR FOSTER CREIGHTON

(1883-1968)

who served at the 1897 Centennial Exposition
and built the present Parthenon building.

Inscription on a bronze tablet near the West Entrance:

The world's only replica of the Parthnon, epitome of Greek culture, was the central building at Tennessee's Centennial Exposition, May 1 thru October 31, 1897. The original temple dedicated to Athena, Greek goddess of wisdom, occupied the most sacred area in Ancient Greece, the crest of the Acropolis, a hill overlooking Athens.

Major Eugene C. Lewis, Director of the Centennial, believed that a reproduction of the Greek masterwork to serve as a gallery of fine arts would inspire a love of beauty and a spirit of excellence. Colonel William C. Smith served as architect and George J. Zolnay, sculptor. Contractor for the building was Edward Laurent with Foster and Creighton contracting for the foundation.

The reception of the Centennial—it was the first exposition in the nation to be both an artistic and financial success—and the public response to the Parthenon indicated that, although it was made with temporary materials, it should be reconstructed on a permanent basis. Construction was started in 1921. The exterior completed in 1925, but due to the lack of funds, it was not until May 20, 1931, that the Parthenon as it stands today was opened to the public.

Hart, Freeland and Roberts, with William Dinsmoor consulting, served as architects; George A. Zolnay, Leopold Scholz, sculptors; Foster and Creighton were general contractors. Others who contributed to the work were John J. Early Company, General Bronze Corporation, John Bouchard and Sons, Herbrick and Lawrence, H. E. Parmer, J. J. Hutchinson and Son, J. O. Kirkpatrick, Charles A. Howell, Art Mosaic and Tile Company, and A. Kanaday.

Board of Park Commissioners

Robert M. Dudley	W. R. Cole	Percy Warner
Edwin Warner	N. T. Bryan	Robert T. Creighton
Rogers Caldwell	C. A. Craig	Lee J. Loventhal
Charles W. W. Cabe	J. P. W. Brown	

This building is listed in the National Register of Historic Places.

FOREWORD

The honor in writing this foreword does not come from dealing with the treasure trove of architectural scholarship and its relation to current and ancient history.

The author, through his own broad knowledge and experience, has handled these matters superbly.

The singular privilege derives, for the writer, from the ability to point out that the world now comes to Nashville to study the Parthenon in the wholeness of its beauty after the original in Greece has been ravaged by the erosion of time and the ruthless vandalism of Man.

It is a replica, yes. But defying all laws of grammar, we will call it "an exact" replica, so true to detail has been its reproduction and so renowned its presence.

The first temple at Nashville, erected of temporary material, was designed as a centerpiece for the Tennessee Centennial Exposition by Colonel W. C. Smith under the supervision of Eugene C. Lewis. The year was 1895.

Wilbur F. Creighton watched the construction as a youth. Then, when the City decided to make the Grecian masterpiece permanent, he was given the assignment in the early Twenties.

Nearly a century has attested to the sound artistry and craftsmanship of this native family of builders. Now W. F. Creighton has written in his own words the story of keeping alive in concrete and stone a structure whose lines spell out the eternal laws of true symmetry and balanced splendor.

The name of Creighton already is preserved on the skyline of Nashville, but the Parthenon in Centennial Park will remain always as a monument to the ability and civic dedication of one of the city's illustrious families.

Charles Moss
Executive Editor
Nashville Banner

PREFACE TO FIRST EDITION

A few months ago I had occasion to visit the Parthenon in Centennial Park. As I drove up I noticed several empty school busses from neighboring counties. Inside the building there were several hundred children wandering around that empty room. There were teachers present but they seemed as idle as the students. As I was the only man living who had a close contact with the construction of the Parthenon, I decided to write a brief, personal story of building the Parthenon in words that children could understand, and to have it printed in a cheap edition which they could afford to buy.

Thousands of tourists visit the ancient ruins in Athens, Greece, and more 200,000 visit the only full scale replica in Nashville annually. They come from every state in the Union and most countries of the world.

This international interest proves to me that the Parthenon occupies a unique place in the interest and affection of the people of the world. Trained architects are interested, because it is a perfect example of the Doric Order of Architecture, and historians and archaeologists are interested because of its historical lore. It is not easy to understand the interest and affection held by the public, except that it is man's highest creation in Art, and Art is a part and parcel of our daily lives.

Children of every civilized nation are taught the history of this ancient temple. Those in Middle Tennessee can study an exact replica.

Wilbur F. Creighton, Sr.

PREFACE TO REVISED EDITION

The 1968 edition was written largely from memory by Wilbur F. Creighton, Sr., edited by Leland R. Johnson, and published by Wilbur F. Creighton, Jr. By providing children and students with basic information about the original Parthenon and Nashville's replica, it proved useful and enjoyed a wide circulation during several printings.

This revised edition was edited and enlarged by Wilbur F. Creighton, Jr. Information and clarifications secured since 1968 have been inserted in the text and materials added concerning the history of Nashville's replica since 1968. Like the first edition, this edition aims at providing basic information about the original temple and the replica for children and students. Many other fine publications are available to those seeking fuller accounts of the subject.

When preparing this revision, the editors received assistance and information from several friends and have extended personal thanks to them. Major contributions came from Parks Director James H. Fyke, Wesley Payne, Anne F. Roos, patron of the Athena Parthenos replica and former member of the Park Board, Susan Wiltshire, Professor of Classics, Vanderbilt University, Barbara Tsakirgis, Associate Professor of Classics, Vanderbilt University, and Alan LeQuire, sculptor.

Wilbur F. Creighton, Jr.
Leland R. Johnson

Parthenon Staff List

Wesley Paine
Director

Marianne Hillenmeyer
Historian

Barry Young
Facility Manager

Vechelle Brown
Gift Shop Assistant

Timothy Cartmell
Gift Shop Manager

Lori Bryant
Front Desk Clerk

Lila Hall
Assistant Curator and Registrar

Nancy Oertel
Secretary

Dee Gee Lester
Education Coordinator

Andrea Carey
Director—Parthenon Patrons

Parks Administration

James H. Fyke
Director

Curt Garrigan
Park Planning

Mary Wherry
Assistant Director—Recreation

Janet Clough
Supt. of Recreation—Arts

Ruins of the Parthenon in Athens

ORIGINAL TEMPLE

The ruined temple standing on the Acropolis in Athens, Greece, of which the Parthenon in Nashville is a full scale replica, was built during the Golden Age of Pericles. Under his wise administration, Greece reached the pinnacle of art and commerce. The painted pottery, sculpture, architecture, drama, music, philosophy, and democratic government developed during those times are still admired.

In pagan times when the temple was built, it was used to worship Athena Parthenos, the Greek virgin goddess of wisdom and the arts of peace. Mythology credited her with giving Athenians the olive tree and inventing tools such as the potter's wheel. Greek history, from the beginning, records the cult worship of Athena (origin of the name

The Acropolis

Athens) on the Acropolis and that at one time a temple built of limestone almost as large as the existing ruins existed.

To celebrate victories, Greek women for centuries donated their golden ornaments. These were fashioned into thin sheets to drape the 42-foot high ivory statue of Athena that adorned the sanctuary in the temple. Sculptured by the famous Phidias, this statue was considered his greatest achievement.

Construction of the temple began in 447 B.C. under the direction of Ictinus, the Architect, and his superintendent, Callicrates. In nine years it was ready for the dedication to the goddess. To a modern builder, this appears a remarkable achievement when it is remembered that these early builders had only man, horse, and oxen power to help. This makes one wonder whether the art of construction has progressed much. The Greek builders, however, had unlimited manpower in the native labor and labor of slaves captured in battle.

◻   ◻   ◻

The Turks captured Athens soon after the fall of Constantinople in 1453. The Parthenon then became a Moslem mosque and had a minaret placed on its roof.

After the Turks were defeated near Vienna in 1683, the Venetians followed up this victory by invading Greece. In 1687, the Venetians besieged a Turkish army that had holed up on the Acropolis. Gunpowder had been stored in the Parthenon's west room, and during the battle a shell burst in it. The resulting explosion wrecked the temple's interior and tumbled much of its exterior ornamentation to the ground.

The temple had been used as a place of religious worship for 2102 years—about 864 as a pagan temple, 1032 years as a Christian church, and 206 years as a Moslem mosque. When the Greeks had converted to Christianity, some say about 336 A.D., the gold and ivory statue of Athena had been sent to Constantinople and it was never heard of again. At first Christians had referred to the temple as Saint Sophia (Hagia Sophia), and later they called it the church of "Our Lady of Athens." The fact that the building was in such good condition at the time of its destruction, after 2,000 years of use, attests to the perfection of design, craftsmanship, and materials used in its original construction.

Nashville's Replica and the Centennial

The origin of the Parthenon's replica in Nashville can be traced to Tennessee's celebration of its centennial as a state during the 1890s. Tennessee entered the Union in 1796, and as its centennial approached in 1896 planning began for a celebration that was to produce the full scale replica of the Parthenon. The history of this centennial celebration therefore is related to the history of the temple's replica.

On August 10, 1892, Douglas Anderson, a member of the Nashville Bar, wrote a letter to a dozen or more newspapers in Tennessee suggesting that an Exposition be held in Nashville to celebrate in 1896 the 100th

Col. William C. Smith, Architect

anniversary of the state's admission to the Union. His recommendation received favorable comment, but nothing was done. The country then was entering an economic depression. Wages and salaries were reduced to a bare living necessity; investment capital was in hiding; there was no construction work. The unemployed were fed in bread lines and soup kitchens.

Colonel William C. Smith, a Nashville architect, proposed on November 17, 1893, to the Nashville Board of Trade that an effort be made to divert public attention from the depression by "starting an enterprise that would interest them in furthering the interest of the city." This idea was accepted by popular favor in Nashville, and a stock company to be known as the Nashville Tennessee Centennial Exposition Company was organized. With a capital of $500,000, the stock company was authorized to sell shares for $25 each, payable at 25 percent in cash, the balance in ten monthly installments. Nashville's population then was only 100,000 and investments in the stock initially were slow. As late as July 7, 1895, the *Nashville American* headlined its newspaper "Centennial or Not?"

At that critical juncture, Nashville's railroads under the leadership of John W. Thomas and E. C. Lewis made substantial investments in the stock company. The City of Nashville, Davidson County, the State of Tennessee, and the United States government also invested in the stock, with the remainder being purchased by all classes of Nashvillians.

With these funds, the company in 1895 began

construction of the Centennial Exposition on the grounds of the former West Side Race Track. The Centennial's Director General E. C. Lewis chose the prominent engineer Wilbur F. Foster as the Director of Works and Foster's business partner Robert T. Creighton as chief of engineering.

Casting about for a central theme to highlight Nashville's cultural history as the "Athens of the South," Major E. C. Lewis hit upon the concept of centering the Exposition around a full scale replica of the Parthenon of Ancient Greece. Winning approval from the company, Lewis employed Colonel William C. Smith as the architect for the replica of the temple. On October 8, 1895, the cornerstone of the replica was laid with appropriate Masonic rites, initiating construction of the temple and also of what was to become known as the "White City."

Major Lewis at the Centennial entertaining visitors in front of the Parthenon

7

*Wilbur F. Foster, Chief Engineer of the Centennial
Exposition, 1897*

*Robert Thomas Creighton, builder and civil engineer, in
charge of buildings and grounds at the Centennial*

Centennial Departments and Buildings

For management of the Centennial Exposition,
sixteen departments were established. These and their
chiefs were:

1. Grounds and Buildings—Robert T. Creighton,
   Engineer in charge;
2. Bureau of Promotion and Publicity—Herman Justi,
   chief;
3. Fine Arts—Theodore Cooley, chief;
4. Commerce and Manufactures—J. H. Bruce, chief;

5. Agriculture, Horticulture and Farm Implements—T.
   F. P. Allison, chief;
6. Machinery—George Reyer, chief;
7. Transportation—A. H. Robinson, chief;
8. Electricity—J. W. Braid, chief;
9. Geology, Minerals and Mining—James M. Safford,
   chief;
10. Forestry and Forest Products—A. E. Baird, chief;
11. Hygiene, Medicine and Sanitary Appliances—Dr. J.
    D. Plunket, chief;
12. Live Stock, Pet Animals, Poultry and Fish—Vanleer
    Kirkman, chief;
13. Military—Adj. Gen. Charles Sykes, chief;
14. Education—Dr. William L. Dudley, chief;
15. Children—W. T. Davis, chief;
16. Negro—Richard Hill, chief.

These departments formed comprehensive divisions
of Tennessee's education, history, industries, health,
social relations, and culture. The buildings constructed on
the grounds also reflected the broad scope of the
Exposition's planning. These buildings, along with their
architects and builders to the extent known, are listed
below.

Building and Type	Architect	Builder
Administration Modern (1890s)	C. A. Asmus	
Agriculture Renaissance	Jul. G. Zwicker	
Auditorium Colonial	Geo. W. Thompson	R. B. McCollom

Children's Roman	F. W. Kreider	
Commerce Roman	B. J. Hodge & Bro.	Hughes & Rives
Education Renaissance	Wm. C. Smith	
Entrance, Main Egyptian	Wm. C. Smith	
Flagstaff 250 feet high	Eugene C. Lewis	
History Greek	Wm. C. Smith	E&N Manufacturing
Knoxville Classic	Albert Bauman	Galyon & Seddon
Machinery Greek	Thompson & Zwicker	Chas. Watterson
Memphis Egyptian	Chas. B. Cook	
Mineral & Forestry Roman-Doric	Gibel & Gabler	
Negro Spanish Renaissance	Frederick Thompson	
Parthenon Greek	Wm. C. Smith	Edward Laurent
Foundation *Rialto* Venetian	Foster & Creighton C. A. Asmus	
Terminal Roman	Wm. C. Smith	
Transportation Renaissance	Jul. G. Zwicker	C. S. Lillie Co.
U.S. Government Classic	Wm. M. Aiken	Geo. Moore & Sons
Woman's Colonial	Sarah Ward Conley	Geo. Moore & Sons

Centennial Exhibits

The buildings were filled with exhibits from Tennessee cities and counties, other states, manufacturers, and other sources. Paintings from around the world, including many by the old masters, were collected for display. Some 1175 works of art made it the largest art exhibition held in the South to that date.

In the Agriculture building, all forms of machinery needed to plant, cultivate, and harvest every farm product grown in Tennessee were displayed. The most modern methods of milking cows, making butter, hatching and raising chickens, and other farming activities were demonstrated.

In the Machinery building, boilers, engines, and generators in operation were displayed. As electricity then was coming into common use, this display proved quite popular. Electric lights also outlined the Exhibition buildings at night and illuminated the grounds.

The Mineral and Forestry building showed every form of mineral commercially mined in Tennessee and illustrated the uses industry made of them. The Barry Vermont Granite Quarries sent a long granite shaft to the display that still stood a century later at the south end of the lake in Centennial Park.

In the Transportation building were exhibited every form of transportation from ox carts to the latest complete passenger train. It included Locomotive 107, the newest then owned by the N.C. & St.L. Railroad.

*A popular amusement of the 1897 Centennial was the
"Giant See-Saw" designed by Nashville engineer Art J.
Dyer. Its two cabs raised terrified groups about 200 feet
above the ground, allowing a good view of the surrounding
country.*

13

View of Centennial Grounds from Giant See-Saw

Many bands played concerts afternoons and nights, six days a week, in the Auditorium. There, too, distinguished civic leaders and prominent historians lectured on Tennessee's history.

Exhibits in the other buildings were instructive and interesting. A spectator could find items of interest for a day's study in each building.

The places of amusement where the visitors spent their money were on the midway, called "Vanity Fair." It had an international flavor.

There were the Streets of Cairo where a camel could be ridden for a small fee, or a man could hire an Egyptian barber to give him a shave beginning with the head and continuing to the feet. A snake charmer mystified the beholders with feats of magic, and donkeys were there for children to ride.

In the Cuban village, pretty, black haired, short skirted young women did what then were thought naughty dances and therefore were popular with male visitors.

The Chinese village was of little interest, but it could be seen through the windows that it was crowded with Chinese. The author suspected the village was used to smuggle Chinese laborers into this country.

The "Chute the Chute" was a long, steep slide where a boat containing several visitors could slide rapidly down into a pool of water. Another popular amusement was the "Giant See-Saw" designed by Nashville engineer Art J. Dyer. Its two cabs raised terrified groups about 200 feet above the ground, allowing a good view of the surrounding country with the never-forgotten doubt of the way to reach the ground if the mechanism failed. Once, it did, and the group aboard remained suspended in the air all night.

Six Venetian gondolas with native gondoliers were brought from Venice. For a small price, a visitor could imagine herself on the canals of that island city while being pushed around Lake Watauga.

At infrequent intervals the State Militia simulated sham battles in an open lot just east of the Exposition. It was exciting to see a field cannon drawn by four horses with two riders gallop over a rough terrain while the two gunners sat with arms folded on a small seat. It was against regulations for them to hold on with their hands. When it came to a stop, the riders turned the piece around to a firing position and one rider held the horses while the other three fired the cannon. The smoke and noise from firing cannon and rifles made these exciting spectacles.

At dark every night, a magnificent fireworks display lasted an hour or more. A recognizable face of a prominent man in a forty-foot high frame would be lit up. Memories of these displays remained with the people who saw them throughout their lives.

Design and Construction of the First Replica

Major Eugene C. Lewis, a consulting civil engineer, was given leave of absence by the DuPont Company and the Louisville and Nashville Railroad, two of his clients, to accept the responsibility of Director General for the Centennial Exposition. A better qualified person could not have been found. A man of strong convictions and a lover of beauty, Lewis had the creative mind and determination required to carry out his ideas.

Three months after construction of the Exposition grounds and buildings began, the engineer in charge resigned, and my father, Robert Thomas Creighton, was offered the position. He was a civil engineer and successful builder. Because of the depression, there was no construction work underway elsewhere, and he was pleased to accept the job, although the salary offered was hardly sufficient to support a family of seven. It became his duty to supervise the construction of the Parthenon replica.

With the mutual respect Major Lewis and my father had for each others' abilities, they made a fine team. They directed completion of the Exposition's buildings and facilities in a short time and within the estimated cost, as was shown in the auditor's report made when the Exposition closed.

Major Lewis conceived the idea of reproducing the Parthenon at the Centennial Exposition to house fine paintings and many other works of art. At his request, the King of Greece sent him copies of the drawings and pictures of the ruins and reports made by commissions that had completed architectural and archaeological studies of the ruins.

The most accurate drawings were those made by Jacques Carrey in 1674. An artist attached to the French embassy to Turkey, his drawings showed in great detail the frieze carvings and the grouping of the figures in the pediments and are the only authentic drawings made of the original building before it was destroyed. His drawings showed a gap of about forty feet in the center of the group in the east pediment. No one knows how or when this gap occurred, but it may have happened while the Turks had control of Greece. The Carrey drawings are preserved in the National Library in Paris.

Major Lewis commissioned Colonel William C. Smith, a prominent local architect, to make working drawings of the Parthenon under his close supervision. Smith had originally proposed the Exposition in 1893. He commanded the First Tennessee Regiment of the National Guard, and in 1898 he led it to the Philippines during the Spanish-American War, where he died of a stroke in the field while on active service.

Sculptors were employed to make models for the building's ornamentation, and they were given the Carrey drawings and information sent by the King of Greece as guidance. To simulate the steep climb to the Acropolis in Athens, where the original Parthenon was located, consideration was given to placing Nashville's replica atop a hill west of the Exposition grounds. This idea was abandoned because it was feared the effort needed to climb the hill might discourage visitors. Instead, material excavated from Lake Watauga was piled in a mound ten feet high to afford the building a commanding place on the grounds. The building's cornerstone was laid on October 8, 1895, with impressive Masonic ceremonies before about 5,000 spectators.

The Exposition did not open in 1896 as planned for

two reasons. It was not entirely completed and 1896 was a Presidential election year. It opened on May 1 and closed on October 30, 1897. The total admissions to the exhibition that summer were 1,786,014. At its end, public auditor Frank Goodman reported that receipts were $1,101,285.84 and disbursements were $1,101,246.40, leaving a balance of $39.44. There were additional assets worth about $12,000 received from sales of salvaged materials.

Colonel Smith's suggestion of 1893 thus had borne fruit. The Exposition diverted public attention from the economic depression, as he had predicted. Moreover the disbursement of a million dollars of revenue and the additional traveling expenses paid by visitors stimulated Nashville's economy, launching a prosperous period that continued for a decade.

A thorough history of the Centennial Exposition, edited by Herman Justi, was written by the participants. This book is available at Nashville's libraries and should be consulted for historical details.

Centennial Exposition and Nashville's Parks

As the Exposition closed in 1897, Nashvillians expressed hope that its site would become a public park and that the Parthenon replica would be preserved. In 1901, Nashville's Park Board organized, with five members appointed by Mayor James H. Head: Major E. C. Lewis, Robert M. Dudley, F. P. McWhirter, Ben Lindauer, and Samuel A. Champion. They received no salary, not even payment for transportation when

WILBUR FOSTER CREIGHTON
1883-1968
Builder of the Parthenon in Nashville

conducting park business. When members of the Park Board died or became incapacitated, the other members elected new members with approval from the City Council. This Board proved successful because there was little money or political preference involved in their management of the park system.

Lacking funds to purchase the Exposition grounds, the Park Board first acquired small parks as gifts from city government, not acquiring the Exposition grounds, or present Centennial Park, until late in 1902. Centennial Park came into the system as a gift from Percy Warner, director of the city's public transport system, in an exchange with the city for certain privileges in operating the street railways.

The prominent citizens forming Nashville's Park Board steadily improved the park system during following decades, and turned over a large system to the Metropolitan Board of Parks and Recreation in 1963 at the formation of Metropolitan Nashville and Davidson County government. This Board also conducted an expansive and award-winning parks and recreation program. Centennial Park and the Parthenon, however, remained as centerpieces of the Metropolitan park system.

Second Parthenon Replica

A decade after the Exposition of 1897 closed, the plaster ornamentation of the original replica of the Parthenon building had deteriorated. Complying with public demand, the Park Board repaired it at great expense. By 1920, however, the deterioration of the plaster had continued to the extent that pieces of the figures in the pediments had begun to fall. The Board closed the building for safety reasons and, again at public demand, decided to rebuild the structure with permanent materials. Because marble was too costly, the second replica was constructed principally of reinforced concrete.

Making the Parthenon permanent, 1923

*Russell E. Hart, architect (seated left), and sculptors Belle
Kinney (standing) and her husband Leopold Scholz*

Russell E. Hart, a Nashville architect and authority
on classic architecture, was commissioned to make the
working drawings for the second replica. He later joined
the engineering firm of Hart-Freeland-Roberts. Although
this firm's engineers designed the concrete frame, to Hart
belongs the credit for the research needed to design a
complete full size replica of the ancient temple. He
consulted with William B. Dinsmoor, a New York
archaeologist who had spent much time in Greece
studying the ruins and who probably knew more about the
ancient temple than any person then living.

Hart had the use of the drawings made by Colonel
Smith, the Carrey drawings, information sent by the King
of Greece, and the measured drawings made by Mr. F. C.

Penrose, published in 1851 in *The Principles of Athenian Architecture*. Few errors were found in the dimensions on the early drawings, but many details needed additional research. Not accepting the conclusion, however trivial, of any expert without substantiating research, Hart spent eleven years on his task.

Scenes on the East and West Pediments

The names of the figures and the proper grouping in the west pediment was simple to determine. A knowledge of mythology, the Carrey drawings, and the Elgin marbles supplied the needed information. It shows Athena and Poseidon, god of the seas, ready for battle. Both are armed, standing face to face, with chariots.

The story was told by the ancient Greeks that in the reign of Kekrops, one of the first kings of Athens, a contest was held between Athena and Poseidon to see who would be the city's patron god. Athena was the goddess of wisdom, defense, and the useful arts, and Poseidon the mighty god of the sea and creator of earthquakes. Because neither god would surrender a claim to Athens, they battled on the Acropolis.

Poseidon hurled his trident spear into the rock of the Acropolis and from the hole it made arose a spring of salt water. The spring symbolized the importance of the sea to Athens, and a gift by Poseidon to the city of naval supremacy and dominance in maritime trade, guaranteeing the city's prosperity. His horses represented waves of the sea and their white manes the wave's white caps.

Athena also thrust her spear into the rock of the Acropolis and from the hole it made arose the olive tree. Olives and olive oil were used daily in ancient Greece in preparing foods. In addition, olive oil was used for medicinal purposes and as the base for perfumes and cosmetics. It was ancient Greece's leading export.

Both gifts were of great value to the city. It was judged, however, that Athena's gift was the greater of the two, so Athena became the city's patron goddess and the city took her name as its own.

This grouping on the west pediment was used on both pediments in Nashville's plaster replica of 1897 because it was difficult to properly group the figures in the east pediment. As earlier noted, a forty-foot gap was missing from the Carrey drawings of the original Parthenon's east pediment. Intensive study of history and mythology was necessary to reconstruct the scene on the east pediment. To help, the British museum sent plaster casts of the Elgin marbles. Live models posed so the sculptors could add the missing parts of the statues.

The principal hint of what had been pictured in the missing forty-foot section came from Pausanias, a Greek traveler and historian of the second century A.D. Of the temple's east pediment, he wrote: "What is seen on entering the Temple relates to the birth of Athena." This referred to mythological stories about her brought down by word of mouth from one generation to the next.

Athena was the eldest child of Zeus, king of Greek gods. Zeus had many children by various consorts, both

East Pediment — the birth of Athena

mortal and immortal, but none was born in quite the manner that Athena was.

The story relates that Zeus sat on his Mount Olympus throne in a bad mood. As the god of the sky, he had a stormy temperament and in a bad mood he hurled lightning bolts to earth. In this instance, he had a fistful of lightning bolts in hand and was in a foul temper because he had a splitting headache.

Because of this headache, his wrath was so terrible it frightened even the other gods and goddesses. Hephaestus, god of blacksmithing and metallurgy, tried to cure Zeus's headache. Picking up a metal axe from his forge, he hurled it into Zeus's skull, splitting it wide open. Being immortal, Zeus did not die. Something stranger happened. From the cleft in his skull, out sprang Athena, full grown, wearing a suit of armor. Dropping onto the ground, she shook her spear and danced. All other gods and goddesses were shocked by this bizarre event. Artemis, goddess of the hunt, recoiled in horror. Little Hebe, cupbearer to the gods, raced away in fright. Even Hephaestus was taken aback by Athena's birth. Only Nike, winged goddess of victory, had presence of mind, and she rushed up to crown Athena with a laurel wreath, the symbol of victory.

Athena's birth was strange even for Greek mythology. The myth appears to be allegorical. Athena was the goddess of wisdom, and wisdom is the one creation, or "child," of man that springs, full grown, from the head.

The grouping on the east pediment finally selected in

Nashville created an international furor. The greatest objection was to the position of Zeus. The objectors claimed that Phidias would not have placed him with his back to part of the court. A careful examination of the east pediment shows that the chair in which Zeus sits is placed at an angle to overcome this objection. A more practical reason is that the pediment is only thirty inches deep. If the chair had been placed facing directly east, the legs of the chair and the feet of Zeus would have projected over the cornice.

The arguments finally ended when an Elgin Marble was found that consisted of a footprint, the leg of a chair, and a piece of the cornice in a position similar to that selected in Nashville. The Elgin Marbles mentioned are pieces of the sculptured figures that had fallen from the Parthenon in Athens and were taken to England by Lord

Parthenon nearing completion, 1927

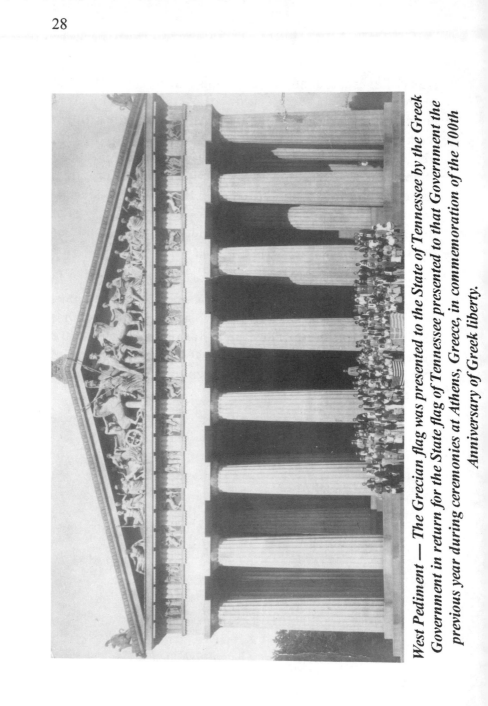

West Pediment — The Grecian flag was presented to the State of Tennessee by the Greek Government in return for the State flag of Tennessee presented to that Government the previous year during ceremonies at Athens, Greece, in commemoration of the 100th Anniversary of Greek liberty.

Elgin, the British Ambassador to Turkey in 1801. He sold them to the British government for about $150,000 and they are displayed in the British Museum.

Identification of West Pediment Characters

Ilissos — personification of an Atenian river god

Krekrops — legendary king of Athens; descendant of Erichithonius, father of Pandrosos, Herse, Aglauros, and Erysichthon.

Pandrosos — legendary princess of Athens

Erysichthon — son of Kekrops

Aglauros — legendary princess of Athens

Erectheus — father of Kekrops, honored in the Erechtheum, another building on the acropolis

Hermes — messenger for the gods

Athcna — goddess of wisdom, warfare, and the useful arts

Poseidon — god of the sea, earthquakes and horses

Iris — messenger for the gods

Amphitrite — Poseidon's consort and charioteer

Kalais — son of Oreithyia and Broeas (north wind)

Oreithyia — daughter of Erectheus

Zetes — son of Oreithyia

Melicertes — son of Ino; became a sea god

Ino — mother of Melicertes; leaped into the sea with her son; both became sea deities

Thalassa — probably an ocean nymph

Cephisos — personification of Athenian river god

Identification of East Pediment Characters

Helios — god of the sun being pulled by four horses that represent the four seasons

Dionysus — god of wine and celebration

Demeter — goddess of grains and fertility - sometimes associated with mother earth

Persephone — daughter of Demeter and wife of Hades, god of the underworld

Iris — messenger for the gods

Poseidon — god of the sea, earthquakes and horses

Hebe — daughter of Hera, cupbearer of the gods, wife of Heracles, goddess of youth

Aphrodite — this figure was once thought to be Aphrodite

Hephaestos — god of fire and metal making, husband of Aphrodite

Zeus — king of the Olympian gods

Nike — goddess of victory

Athena — goddess of wisdom, warfare and the useful arts

Ares — god of war

Artemis — goddess of the hunt

Hera — goddess of marriages, wife of Zeus

Hermes — messenger of the gods

Apollo — god of music and civilization

Ganymede — cup bearer of the gods

Hestia — goddess of the hearth

Dione — mother of Aphrodite

Aphrodite — goddess of love and beauty, mother of Eros (Cupid)

Selene — goddess of the moon with four horses which represent the four seasons

Rebuilding Nashville's Parthenon

My matured interest in Nashville's Parthenon replica began in 1922 when our company received the contract to rebuild the first replica in permanent materials and I was assigned to supervision of its construction. It was an unusual contract because it proceeded only as fast as the Park Board could obtain funds to pay the workmen and Hart, the architect, could complete the work drawings. The eventual result was that more time was used, by a year, in rebuilding the replica than was needed to build the original temple in Athens.

The stone foundations, brick walls around the Cella, and other durable parts of the 1897 replica remained in place during the reconstruction of the 1920s. The stone foundations under the columns, however, were strengthened to help support the heavier, new columns.

I know of no building in history measured and studied more thoroughly by commissions of architects, historians, and archaeologists from nearly every civilized nation than the ruins of the Parthenon at Athens. These are some of the measurements. The length of the upper step of the stylobate, or platform on which the Cella stands, was 228 feet in length, the East step was 101.341 feet and the West step was 101.363 feet which is the Greek standard of length and is equal to the length of one second of latitude at the equator. The body of the building, or Cella, was divided into a smaller and a larger chamber. The smaller, at the west end, was known as the Treasury and contained the sacred vessels and similar items of value. This western room, to which the name Parthenon was first confined, could be entered only through the western doors. The name itself signifies "Chamber of the Virgins," and refers to the daughters of the foremost families of Athens, who carried the peplos, or sacred garment, offered to the goddess at the Panathenaic Festival. The Treasury was only about 44 feet deep with a width of 63 feet, and its ceiling was carried by four columns not of the Doric order. The larger chamber at the eastern end was known as the Naos. Its length was 100 Attic feet, and according to our measurements it had a length of 98 feet and width of 63 feet. Around three sides of this chamber ran a two-storied colonnade of the Doric order. Facing the Eastern and principal entrance to the temple stood the famous chryselephantine statue of the goddess, Athena Parthenos.

For Nashville's permanent replica, the Earley Studios of Washington, DC, took the contract for making casts of the sculptured figures, columns, and other ornamentations, using the Earley process. Briefly, this used a mixture of carefully selected sand and crushed gravel and the best cement. This mixture was poured into rubber molds lined with tin foil, and when it hardened the molds were removed and the surfaces rubbed by skilled plasterers with steel brushes. Uniformity of color was obtained with a weak acid solution. The column drums were cast in four sections about five feet high and eight inches thick and were anchored to the reinforced concrete columns supporting the roof.

Earley produced the desired colors by using Potomac River gravel mixed with crushed colored ceramic tile and cement. The work of Earley's craftsmen when executing

George Zolnay, sculptor for the Metopes in 1897 and 1925

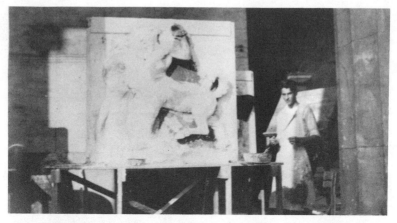

Jack Shwab, assistant to Zolnay, working on the Metopes

this intricate work perfectly demonstrated the skill of artisans in the employ of this famous organization.

George Zolnay, the sculptor who had helped make the models for ornamentation of the 1897 building, was retained to make models for the Metopes, or frieze, over the outer colonnade. He had perfected a mortar mixture color to cast the figures in the desired color.

It might be added here that on the original Parthenon the Metopes on the east represented battles between the Gods and the giants. On the west the battle between the Greeks and the Amazons was shown; on the south the Greeks were shown fighting the Centaurs; and on the north the subject was the conquest of Troy.

Belle Kinney, a native sculptress of Nashville, and her husband Leopold Scholz, an Austrian sculptor, were commissioned to make the models for the figures in the pediments. After completing plaster models for the

1931 Parthenon Building

pediment groups, they began work on the full size statues. Plaster casts, made from the priceless marble originals, were shipped from Europe, and these were used to create the molds for the finished versions on the outside of the building. This guaranteed their absolute accuracy. Both the plaster models and the full size casts are now in the museum's permanent collection.

Structural Questions

While experts agreed on the dimensions of the Parthenon's structural features, which had been taken to one thousandth of a foot, their conclusions about some architectural features do not agree. I will mention a few of the conclusions and give my opinion, as a builder, of which arc correct.

The greatest disagreement concerned the proper grouping of the missing figures in the east pediment. How this issue was settled has been previously described.

Opinion differed about the roof over the Sanctuary. Some think it was roofed and the pagan priests depended on torches and light from the seven by twenty-four foot east door. It is said that the pagans did not worship in congregations.

Others agree with this theory, but say that when Christian worship started openings were made in the roof. The Catholic priests needed more light. A painting made prior to the explosion of 1687 shows a raised roof with small windows on each side.

The fact that there is a depressed section in the floor

1923 Reconstruction of the Parthenon

of the Sanctuary, 84.501 by 32.283 feet, extending to the east wall created differences of opinion between the experts. Such a depressed floor section, called an impluvium, is found also in other ancient Greek temples and in Nashville's War Memorial Building.

One reason why Ictinus might have built the impluvium was to hold water. Perhaps the presence of moisture near the statue of Athena could prevent the ivory of Athena's face, arms, and hands from cracking, or perhaps the water reflected light from the doorway into the room and onto the statue of Athena.

There were no straight lines in the building, except perhaps in the wall separating the two rooms. There were no openings in the walls of the original building. The curves used by its builders were not segments of a circle, but of a parabolic or hyperbolic curve.

It is a well known principle of optics that a long horizontal line appears to sag when observed from a distance. That the designers of the Parthenon knew this law is shown if an observer will sight along the top side step. It will be noted that it rises in the center nine inches. This rise is called a camber. The building's eaves and ridge have the same rise. From a distance, they appear to be horizontal.

The same optical illusion causes two parallel vertical lines to appear to diverge or separate as they rise. The Greeks architects found that a column with straight lines from the base to capital had, to the eye, a slightly concave appearance. This they counteracted by giving the columns a slight convexity or bulge, know technically as "entasis." The axes of the columns are not at right angles to the floor but lean inward slightly, nearly 3 inches in their total height of 34 feet. It has been calculated that these axes, if prolonged skyward, would meet at a common point 5850 feet above the floor. This added the appearance of stability in the building. It also added tremendously to the skill needed to cut the bed joints of the columns, which were horizontal and not at right angles to the center line. It is believed that the Greeks built the columns with projected center lines meeting at one focal point as an expression of their belief in a Supreme Being.

The four corner columns are slightly thicker than the others because, outlined against the sky, they would appear to be of slightly smaller diameter than those seen against the darker background of the walls. The columns vary in width from one to another, and they are not spaced an equal distance apart as they appear to be. The spacing varies from 15.531 feet to 14.066 feet. Just think of the increased work needed to cut the lintels to the correct lengths caused by these different spacings.

Another dispute concerns how the colors were applied as a background for the Metopes, the pediments, and in the interior. If they had been painted on they would have faded in time. Although some scholars think the statues were once painted, an official of the British Museum wrote me that he saw no evidence that the Elgin Marbles had ever been painted.

It is known that the art of burning brilliant colors in terra-cotta was at a high state of perfection in ancient times, and I have read that this art was lost in the fall of Rome. It is thought by some that the red background of the Metopes was inlaid terra-cotta.

There are many more of these unresolved questions. None of them seem significant to me as a builder and are only mentioned to show the great care and skill used by our workmen in adhering to these intricate dimensions to a tolerance of one-eighth inch.

Construction Methods

As I learned more about the Parthenon's structure I began to wonder what methods were used by its ancient builders to quarry, transport, carve, and set in place the heavy column drums and the lintels over them, which if

Elgin marble cast, male figure

they were in one piece weighed twenty tons. I am sure that all ornamentations were cut roughly to size, set in place, and then carved from scaffolds after the building was occupied. Many experts agree that the carving was not completed until 432 B.C.

That the Greeks were perfectionists is shown by the fact that the backs of sculptured figures, which are not visible from the ground, are as perfectly carved as the fronts.

Elgin marble cast, female figure

I make no claim to being an art critic, but even I appreciate the perfect carving of faces which seem ready to speak, the perfect emphasis of male muscles and the delicate folds of the women's draperies. It will be noticed that females are shown entirely clothed and that males are shown in the nude.

Solving the problem of the method used to raise and set the heavy stone was most intriguing. It is a simple task today with blocks and falls, cranes, and mechanized equipment. In ancient times it would have been difficult.

The encyclopedia says the principle of increased power through the multiple pulley was discovered by Archimedes, a famous Greek mathematician who died 226 years after the Parthenon was built. If this is true, the builders of the Parthenon used only the single pulley. With a single pulley, the pull on the line is equal to the weight to be lifted. Archimedes learned that if the line is passed through additional pulleys, the pull may be many times less than the weight to be raised.

Scholar William Dinsmoor wrote: "For hoisting and placing, tongs worked with pulleys and derricks usually gripped bosses left on the exposed surfaces, which could then be set on their final beds almost in the exact position, requiring no blocking or use of a crowbar." This is the way heavy stones are placed today.

There is no doubt that the early Greek builders used tongs or hooks, as well as lewises, to raise lighter stone, but the records show that two circular stone ribs were left around a rectangular shaped stone, showing that it was intended to be rolled into place and lowered with crow bars, after which the ribs were cut off. Dinsmoor had been so thorough in his research, however, that I could not discard his description of construction methods without considerable thought.

Experts agree that the Pentelic marble used in the ancient Parthenon came from a quarry located about fifteen miles from Athens. This stone is a white color, close grained, and breaks in a straight line. Methods used to quarry this stone were doubtless much the same as those used today except holes in the stone then were drilled by hand instead of by compressed air machines. The stone was sawed to a straight line by hand, using a thin, wrought iron blade worked back and forth over hard sand and water.

Experts also agree that the stone was hauled from the quarry on low wagons pulled by twenty to thirty oxen. This many oxen were needed to pull the heavy load up the steep hill of the Acropolis.

While rebuilding Nashville's Parthenon during the 1920s, I asked our two most experienced stone setters how they would raise the heavy lintels to the tops of the columns without the use of blocks and falls or mechanized equipment. They gave the problem great thought and finally they agreed. The only way would be to build a heavy wooden ramp as high as the top of the columns and carry the stones up the ramp on the same wagon that had brought them from the quarry, then roll or pry them into place with crow bars.

Finally, I remembered that the Greeks were great sailors and that sailors used a capstan to raise a ship's

Largest bronze doors in the world.
Each leaf weighs 7.5 tons.

anchors. A capstan is a windlass on a vertical shaft, and it has recesses in its top into which heavy poles are placed. Men pushing on these poles while walking in a circle could wind an anchor cable around the windlass. If the anchor were caught below a ledge of stone, a very strong pull would have been needed to raise the anchor.

Greek engineers had great technical skill. For example, they embedded wrought iron rods in the stone masonry and cantilevered them out to take the weight of the figures in the pediments off the cornice below. Certainly they could have designed a capstan strong enough, with the power of many men, to have raised the stone and then set it in place with the help of "gin poles." A gin pole is a strong pole, guyed to the ground with cables, with its top leaning enough to clear the load. With cables passing through single pulleys fastened to the top of gin poles, a capstan windlass could have raised and set the stones as Dinsmoor described it being done.

It must be admitted that Dinsmoor prepared a marvelous design for the interior of Nashville's Parthenon in 1927. The design included strips of metal built into the walls from which fine paintings could have been suspended for display. The interior design was so perfectly proportioned, however, that some people thought exhibited paintings would detract from its beauty. From 1931 to the 1990s, the interior remained empty except for small scale models of the figures in the pediments and plaster casts of the Elgin Marbles. Over the years I took friends with little interest in classical history to visit the building. I observed, however, that with no prompting

The Parthenon's columns lean toward the center of the building. See the "Grecian Urn" at the end of the Exterior Porch.

each removed his hat on entering the building as if entering a church or temple.

Parthenon Renovation, 1986-1988

By 1986 some of the building's service and support areas had become obsolete and inadequate. It hosted more than 170,000 visitors annually, served as the City Art Gallery, and continued as the centerpiece of Centennial Park. The Metropolitan Board of Parks and Recreation therefore approved upgrading the building's facilities to better serve its staff and the increasing numbers of visitors. To solve various problems with the aging building and to introduce new spaces in support of the building's expanding role, the Board selected the Nashville-based architectural firm of Gresham, Smith and Partners.

This firm spent a year studying the building and planning its renovation, calling on the expertise of architects, engineers, foundation and soils scientists, museum consultants, and a statuary conservator. This team designed unique solutions for the structural challenges. Included in the final design were upgraded staff facilities, curatorial areas, a new gift shop, and a new handicapped accessible main entrance. Improved fire safety features, emergency exits, and new public facilities were provided. Central to the design was the renovated City Art Gallery, housing the Cowan art collection. Also provided were interpretive areas highlighting Nashville's Centennial Exposition of 1897, Nashville's Parthenon, and the original Parthenon in Athens.

These improvements were provided without destroying the building's architectural integrity by placing

48

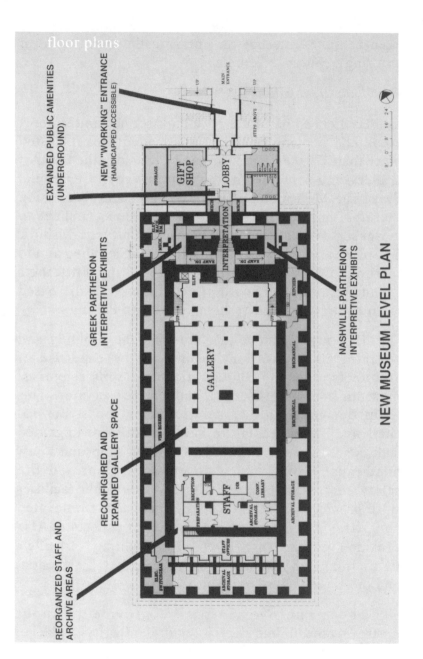

floor plans

EXPANDED PUBLIC AMENITIES (UNDERGROUND)

NEW "WORKING" ENTRANCE (HANDICAPPED ACCESSIBLE)

GREEK PARTHENON INTERPRETIVE EXHIBITS

NASHVILLE PARTHENON INTERPRETIVE EXHIBITS

RECONFIGURED AND EXPANDED GALLERY SPACE

REORGANIZED STAFF AND ARCHIVE AREAS

STORAGE

GIFT SHOP

LOBBY

MAIN ENTRANCE

UP

UP

STEPS ABOVE

INTERPRETATION

RAMP DN.

RAMP DN.

MEDL.

ELEC. MACH. RM.

ELEV.

UP

UP

KITCHEN

MECHANICAL

MECHANICAL

GALLERY

FIRE RISERS

RECEPTION

PREPARATION

STAFF

LIB.

CONF. LIBRARY

ARCHIVAL STORAGE

ARCHIVAL STORAGE

STAFF OFFICES

ELEC. SWITCHGEAR

ARCHIVAL STORAGE

NEW MUSEUM LEVEL PLAN

0'   8'   16'   24'

49

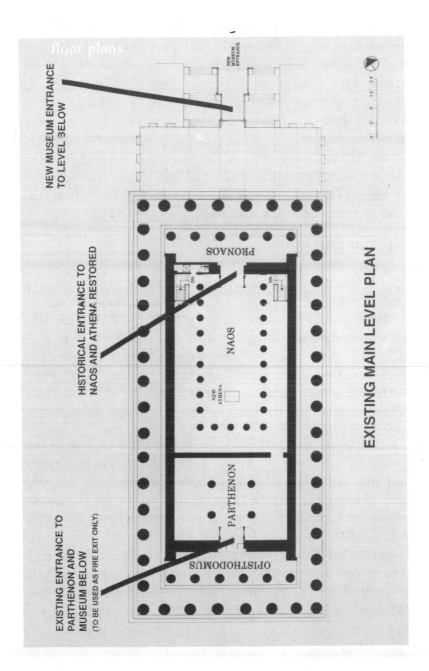

floor plans

NEW MUSEUM ENTRANCE
TO LEVEL BELOW

NEW MUSEUM ENTRANCE

HISTORICAL ENTRANCE TO
NAOS AND ATHENA RESTORED

EXISTING ENTRANCE TO
PARTHENON AND
MUSEUM BELOW
(TO BE USED AS FIRE EXIT ONLY)

PRONAOS

NAOS

NEW ATHENA

PARTHENON

OPISTHODOMUS

EXISTING MAIN LEVEL PLAN

new developments underground adjacent to the basement and using the space beneath the porches. The interpretive areas were placed on the ramp network installed to provide barrier-free access to the building, and a handicapped-accessible elevator was placed in a space between two walls. These measures minimized the impact on the historic structure and the vistas of the building from the surrounding park, and the resulting modifications were acclaimed by the historical and architectural communities as well as the public at large.

Athena Parthenos

While the renovation was underway, the sculpting and erecting of a replica of Athena Parthenos, the statue that occupied the interior of the ancient Parthenon, was also undertaken. Phidias sculpted the original statue at Athens in nine years, and his chryselephantine (ivory and gold) creation was regarded as a masterpiece. The Phidian sculpture disappeared in ancient times, however, leaving small models and pictures on coins to indicate its splendor.

Although support existed for placing a replica of the Phidian Athena in Nashville's Parthenon, its Sanctuary remained impressively barren until the 1980s. The Board of Parks and Recreation knew the cost of the replica statue would be high and other park system needs seemed more pressing. When Sculptor Puryear Mims in 1974 proposed to create an Athena statue, however, the Board placed a donation box at the Parthenon to collect public contributions for the purpose. During following years, these contributions so increased that by the 1980s it appeared possible to initiate the replica's production.

New West entrance, 1989

52

Anne F. Roos, a Board member and civic leader, investigated the known images of the original Athena and contacted scholars studying the subject. These included Neda Leipen, Curator of the Greek and Roman Department of the Royal Ontario Museum, Brunilde Sismondo Ridgway, Professor of Classical and Near Eastern Archaeology at Bryn Mawr College, and Professor Evelyn B. Harrison of New York University's Institute of Fine Arts. Professors Ridgway and Harrison had been students of William Bell Dinsmoor and knew of Nashville's Parthenon.

Information from these sources indicated that a full scale replica, about forty feet tall, of Athena Parthenos could be produced, if a sculptor of sufficient ability and determination could be located. The Board in early 1982 requested proposals for the task from Tennessee sculptors. After reviewing the several proposals received, the Board assigned the task to Alan LeQuire, a young sculptor from Nashville who studied in Europe and had completed several works of art in the city.

Sculptor LeQuire visited Athens to measure the space occupied by the original statue's base and to examine surviving images of Phidias's monumental creation. Work then began in a Nashville warehouse, creating a small scale model and moulding several tons of clay into the proper image. LeQuire had the support of several assistants and of more than fifty volunteers over a period of seven years. Because Nashville could not afford a statue of ivory and gold like the original, and to reduce the statue's weight, LeQuire selected a fiberglass and gypsum cement mixture to form the statue's exterior.

*Sculptor Alan LeQuire completes the clay feet and base of
the statue of Athena in preparation for final casting*

Two problems soon appeared. The weight of the giant statue could place a severe stress on the building's structure. At about forty-two feet high, the Athena would become the largest indoor statue in the world—more than a third the size of the Statue of Liberty. Moreover the cost of a statue of this size soon exceeded available funding.

In its customary manner, the Nashville community came to the Athena project's assistance. Ben Rechter arranged for the Rogers Group of firms to donate and install a steel framework from the Parthenon's foundation rock extending through the art gallery in the basement and into the Sanctuary, providing a secure support and armature for the statue. Anne F. Roos organized the Athena Fund Foundation to obtain state, corporate, and private contributions towards the statue's creation, and by 1989 individual and corporate contributions of both services and funding had nearly assured the project's completion. Additional funds will have to be raised to make the gilding of the statue a reality.

When the Parthenon closed for renovation in 1987 and 1988, Alan LeQuire and his assistants began assembling the cast pieces of the statue on its steel armature, and the white Carrara marble to serve as its base was ordered. By 1989 the statue had reached its full height and the detailed artwork on the shield and other finishing touches were in progress.

As LeQuire sculpted, scholars put together fragmentary evidence to reveal the statue's details. Athena's shield, fifteen feet in diameter, has 31 Greek and Amazon figures in relief with the Parthenon, Acropolis,

Standing some fifteen feet in diameter, Athena's shield is a complex sculpture in its own right. On the exterior in high relief is a depiction of Greek heroes and amazons savagely contesting an unnamed city. In the Greek mind, the amazons were symbols of other cultures, especially the Persians, whom the Greeks considered barbarians. In the Greek myth, the amazons lived in the area of Eastern Anatolia, and the long robes and effeminate manners of the Persians were likened to those of the legendary women warriors. In the center of the shield is the grotesque image of Medusa, slain by Perseus with the help of Athena. As a thanks for offering her help, Perseus gave the Gorgon's head to the goddess, who put it on her shield as a protective device. The Medusa appears on Athena's breastplate.

and walls of Athens behind the figures. On Athena's breast, she wears the aegis bearing the head of Medusa surrounded by snakes, a gift from Zeus to protect her from her enemies by turning them into stone. On the sandals are Centaurs and Lapiths. Her helmet has a Sphinx in the center and winged horses at each side with trailing plumes. In Athena's right hand is a Nike, a winged Victory, that is six feet and four inches tall. On the base is a sculpture of the birth of Pandora, the mythological first woman. The original statue had garments of gold and ivory worth millions of dollars in today's prices. Nashville's replica will have gold leaf on the garments and armor. The skin surfaces will be painted.

Just as the Parthenon building was designed to compensate for optical illusions, so is the Athena replica. The statue's proportions are generally more massive than human proportions and optical corrections have been made by the sculptor. To prevent the head of the forty-two foot replica from appearing tiny when viewed from the floor, all the statue's proportions are expanded from the waist upwards. The head and shoulders are much larger than they would have been if in human proportion with the legs and feet.

Anne Roos wrote the following account of the history of Nashville's Athena:

> The study of World History will always include the Classical Age of Greece as one of the most interesting, successful and influential chapters in the history of mankind. Nashville citizens chose to recreate the fabled Parthenon because it represented a pinnacle achievement in mankind's

odyssey. Since the late 19th century, we have had this beautiful building as a mirror in which to see ourselves in surroundings that represent another great era in Western Civilization. History has been made vivid to countless adults and school children that have had the good fortune to walk along the columns of its porticos.

The curiosity is aroused about the rest of the story that played to the citizens of Athens 400 years before Christ. The Parthenon was built to house the colossal statue of Athena who was the patron goddess of the Athenians. The Parthenon "experience" as we have had it until now is incomplete without the statue. There is a great deal of speculation about how the scale worked in the building. Did the proportions of the figure affect the architectural decisions? How did the details, such as the Lapiths and Centaurs that decorated the soles of Athena's sandals really look? How did the great shield with its 31 warriors and Amazons appear when it rested by Athena's side? We will soon be closer to answering all these questions and many more.

The focus also shifts to the amazing work of the archaeologists who have fitted together information from unearthed fragments, ancient models and travelogues, to give us a very complete idea of how the statue must have looked. Indeed, the sculpting of the LeQuire statue of Athena Parthenon precipitated additional research in order that we might have the best possible information for this replica that has attracted the attention of students of the classics world wide.

*The statue of Athena nearing completion with
Alan LeQuire working on the arm*
Photo © Alan LeQuire.

I have been busy answering the question: why
Athena? There is a second part of the question
which is: why Athena now? Eight years ago, in
December 1981, I served on the Board of the Parks
and Recreation Department and felt strongly that
it was important to seize the moment if we were to
have the statue for which the Parthenon was built
done at all in the foreseeable future. Seed money
for the project had been donated by visitors to the
Parthenon. Then, when a sculptor was identified
who was courageous and competent and
eminently suited to the project, it seemed crucial
to begin. Alan LeQuire had developed his
considerable talent and ability abroad and was
ready to settle back home in Nashville. He had a
gift for the realistic representation of the human
form and he had the academic interest and
discipline to address the creative problems of the
statue within the framework supplied by
archaeological research. What we could not have
known at the beginning is that he also was
persistent. When the engineering problems
attached to such an undertaking became
horrendous, he set about trying various solutions
until he got it just right.

In addition, at this time in the history of the
Metro Parks, there is a senior staff that are open
to new ideas and interested in supporting the high
cultural profile of the Metro Park system. Jim Fyke
as director, Lallie Richter as superintendent of
park planning and development, and Frank
Atchley as superintendent of all maintenance for
Metro Parks, gave Alan LeQuire a great deal of

back-up support without which the project would
not have been possible. Also, just as with the Dee's
Park Sea Serpent, I could never have seen this
project to completion without the whole hearted
support and considerable problem solving ability
of my husband, Charles E. Roos.

¤   ¤   ¤

Cowan Art Gallery

The Southern people did not recover from the
traumatic effects of the civil war until late in the
nineteenth century. The Tennessee Centennial
Exposition with the Parthenon as a repository for objects
of fine arts emphasized the need for an art museum after
the Centennial closed. Frick, Morgan, Gardner and others
had formed great collections in accordance with the
period's prevailing fascination for things European,
particularly the Old Masters. Yet there were a few
pioneering collectors who looked to their compatriots and
contemporaries. Among this group was James M. Cowan
(1858-1930).

When the Parthenon was being rebuilt in the 1920s a
basement was dug under the entire ground floor to
provide for an Art Gallery. At this time James M. Cowan
offered anonymously a part of his art collection, provided
the Parthenon could be used to house it.

Mr. Cowan had visited the Tennessee Centennial
Exposition as the sponsor of a troup of little girls known
as The Armour Drill Corps of Chicago. He remembered
the pleasant treatment his group received during their
performance at The Exposition and he wanted to do

something to benefit his native state. He had a warm feeling about his boyhood in Cowan, Tennessee, not far from Nashville. Mr. Cowan had in his personal collection nearly 800 pieces of art which were the work of artists born in America or of those who had emigrated to America.

At the time of his death in 1930, he had donated 63 paintings. The collection includes those of Frederick Church, George Inness, Alfred Giestat, Sanford Gifford, Gardner Symons and many others.

Just as the ancient temple in Athens contained the treasures of Athena, the people of Nashville have their own treasure in the Cowan Art Gallery.

Because the cornerstone of Nashville's Parthenon was placed on October 8, 1895, the building completed its first century in 1995. During that century it served the community in many capacities—as a Centennial centerpiece, a gallery for the arts, a stage for grand theatre, and a central recreation site. It became a symbol of the civic aspirations of the "Athens of the South."

The temple's renovation during the 1980s and the addition of the Athena Parthenos replica drew renewed national and international attention to the structure and have prepared it for its second century of service to the community.

Standing above the skyline of the present-day Athens on the Acropolis are the hallowed ruins of the Parthnon.

This building, designed by the architect Phidias in the fifth century B.C., is mute witness to the glory of ancient

Greece, the tattered remains of a society that flourished for 2000 years before Christ and at its glorious age gave the world the very fabric of Art, Science, Philosophy and Democracy. It was the land of Plato, Socrates, and Aristotle, the land of great temples, statues of gods and goddesses of unequaled beauty and perfection. The Parthenon and the statue of Athena represent the most perfect achievement of ancient Greece.

After the desecration of the Parthenon and the loss of the statue of Athena, no one in the world could imagine that the full grandness of the building and the statue would be reborn halfway around the world in Nashville, Tennessee, known as the "Athens of the South."

The Bicentennial Celebration

A special session of the Tennessee State Legislature was called by Governor Don Sundquist to celebrate the state's 200th birthday on June 1, 1996. An hour-long narrative of seven periods in Tennessee's legislative history was the General Assembly's contribution to the Statehood Day celebration. Vice President Albert Gore Jr., Governor Sundquist, former Governor Ned McWherter, Senator Douglas Henry and many others contributed to the discussions.

The real celebration was held in the new Bicentennial Capitol Mall, where more than ten thousand people had gathered on the lawn behind the state capitol, on the Mall and in the 2000-seat amphitheater. The day-long ceremonies included musical performances from some of Tennessee's top entertainers, stirring speeches, uniformed soldiers, roaring jet airplanes, fireworks which

The Bicentennial Capitol Mall

lit up the entire downtown area, and at dusk a twenty-cannon salute marked the close of Statehood Day and the dedication of the Bicentennial Capitol Mall.

Think of how wonderful it would be if a hundred years from now both the Parthenon and the Bicentennial Capitol Mall are alive and well, still providing beauty and pleasure to the citizens of this community.

APPENDIX A — REMODELING THE EXTERIOR COLUMNS OF THE PARTHENON

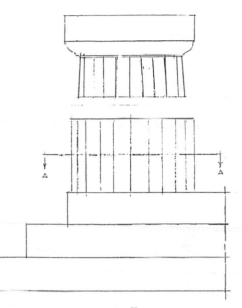

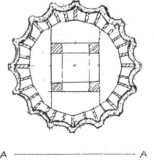

Figure 1

Figure 1

Doric column built in 1897 is approximately 6 feet 2 inches in diameter at the base and 31.25 feet in height. The 2 inch wood ribs are supported by a wood lattice column. These ribs are two inch thick members placed in the flukes as shown and trimmed on the outside to form the delicate curving entasis as the diameter of the column diminishes toward the top. 2.5 inches of wood lath and plaster cover the outside of the column.

Note:

In the present building the six non-loadbearing columns under the porches at the east and west ends have not been changed. The wood lath and lime plaster was removed and the "Earley Process" concrete was placed in the 2.5 inch space. See Figure 4.

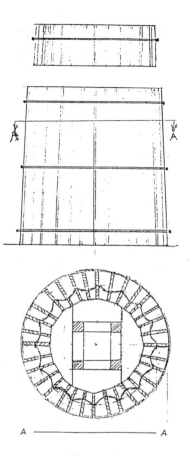

Figure 2

Figure 2

1. The wood lath and lime plaster is removed.
2. Light wire mesh is placed in the outside of the ribs.
3. Two inch wood ribs are placed on each rib cut to the same curvature as the old rib.
4. One inch diameter rods with turn buckles are placed around the outside of the new ribs.

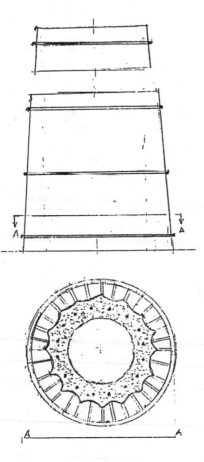

Figure 3

Figure 3

Figure 3

1. Remove the old lattice column leaving the wire mesh attached to the new ribs.
2. Place eight inch reinforced concrete collar: a metal adjustable form used on the inside, The wire mesh serves as a form for the outside (see page 70).

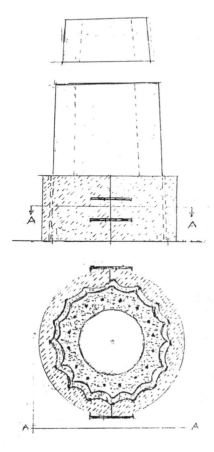

Figure 4

Figure 4

1. Remove the rods and outside ribs.
2. Line the lightwewight removable forms with aluminum foil.
3.Place the form 2.5 inches from the surface of the concrete column.
4. Place special "Earley Process" concrete mix in the 2.5 inch space. The height of this pour is the same as the height of the drum on the Parthenon in Greece.
5. The following day remove the form.
6. Treat the surface by the "Earley Process."

Note:
The "magic" of the process is that while the mixture was in the mould, the rock fragments come to the surface, and when the casting is worked over with a wire brush and steel scraping tool the film of concrete is drawn away and the surface is that of the rock fragments in their natural colors, the "aggregate" as it is called.

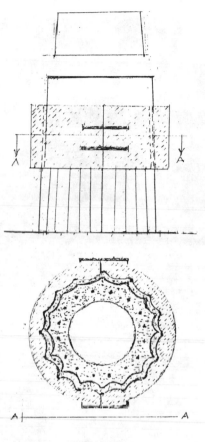

Figure 5

Figure 5

1. Place the form above for the next pour.
2. Adjust to the height of the next drum.

A cross-section of a Parthenon column in 1925, when a reinforced concrete collar replaced the wooden columns built in 1897

APPENDIX B
Erect Bronze Doors

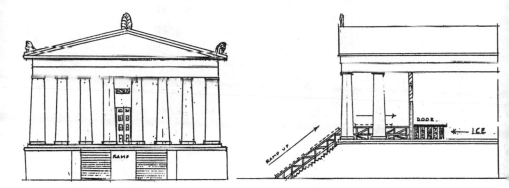

Figure 6

Figure 7

Figure 6

East elevation of Parthenon showing pair of bronze doors — each leaf 23.55 feet high, 6.66 feet wide and 1.08 feet thick, weight 7.5 tons. The wood ramp is built over the steps extending to the door sill.

Figure 7

One leaf of the door is rolled up the ramp into the inside of the building and placed on blocks of ice.

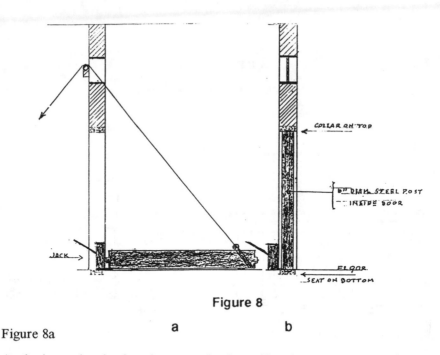

Figure 8

a   b

Figure 8a

As the ice melts, the door lowers to the door sill and rests on the toe of two jacks

Figure 8b

After the bottom of the door is placed on the jacks, the post is placed into the ball bearing seat in the floor and the ball bearing collar is placed on the top and anchored to the wall.

Note:
After the door is hung the post turns on the ball bearing socket in the floor and in the collar at the top and it swings above the floor. The bronze guides in the floor are placed there to resemble those used in the Greek Parthenon to support heavy wooden doors.

APPENDIX C
Wood Beams

From Greek history we know that the timbers for the roof trusses came from the Cedars of Lebanon. Measurements of the ruins indicate the bottom chord of the truss was 2.5 feet wide, 2 feet deep and 63 feet long. In order to get timbers similar to the ones used originally, kiln dried tide water cypress timbers were purchased from the Putnam Lumber Company of Shamrock, Florida. The Kirkpatrick Lumber Company of Nashville milled the members to cover the bottom flange of the structural steel trusses. Due to the length of the span it was necessary to have one splice in the center. When you look up from the floor, you see beams 2.5 feet wide x 2 feet deep and 63 feet long.

APPENDIX D — FRIENDS OF THE LEQUIRE STATUE OF ATHENA PARTHENOS

(to January 1, 1991)

Olympians ($5,000 plus)

Mrs. Florence Cheek Lamb
National Recovery Technologies
Nissan Motor Manufacturing Co.
Mrs. Ruth Puryear
Charles and Anne Roos

The Rogers Group
Ben Rechter
Tennessee Arts Commission
The Tennessee Humanities Council

Champions ($1,000 to $4,999)

Aladdin Indust. Foundation, Inc.
American Institute of Architects
    Middle Tennessee Chapter
Bill Armistead
Ash-McNeil
    Gene McNeil
AVCO
Daniel and Patricia Burton
Cem-Fill
    John Jones
Franklin "Red" Clark
Concrete Form Co.
Mr. Wilbur F. Creighton, Jr.
Mr. & Mrs. Ervin Entrekin
Dr. and Mrs. Ernest G. Fremanis
First American National Bank
Sam Fleming
Gannett Foundation

Mrs. Mildred Green
Gresham and Smith
HCA Park View Medical Center
Hart, Freeland and Roberts
Hellenic Women's Cultural
    Association of Atlanta, Ga.
Senator Douglas Henry, Jr.
Mrs. Kathryn Craig Henry
Heritage Land Co.
Mr. John A. Hill
Bill Hudson and Assoc.
Mr. & Mrs. Walter Knestrick
Dr. & Mrs. Virgil LeQuire
Mr. Donald M. Maillie
McDonald's Mid-Tenn Co-op.
Metro Arts Commission
Nashville Greek Community
The Nashville Banner/Tennessean

Opryland U.S.A., Inc.
Drs. Titus and Mary Podea
    New York, NY
Dr. Carlton Roos
Drs. Sarah and Gordon Sell
Tenn. Classical Association
Dept. of Classical Studies,
    Vanderbilt University
Tenn. Teachers Credit Union
Dr. & Mrs. John B. Thomison

Carolyn Tune
Tune Entrekin and White
U.S. Gypsum
    Ed Love
Wallboard and Supply
    G. G. Waggoner
Mrs. Mary Pope Whitson
    McMinnville, TN
Mrs. Mary H. Witherspoon

Heroes ($500 to $999)

Mr. & Mrs. Charles Allen
Allen Investments
Bernal Foundation
Commerce Union Bank
Webb Follin
Mr. & Mrs. Wm. L. Fowler
Gale Smith Insurance Co.
    John A. Witherspoon, Jr.
Mrs. B. B. Gullett
Mrs. Mary T. Hobbs
Mrs. Nancy W. Howell
Cloe Fort Lenderman
David and Joyce McCroskey
    Walland, TN

Nashville City Bank
    John Hardcastle
Northern Telecom, Inc.
Dr. Greer Richetson
Mr. Kenneth L. Roberts
Mrs. Margaret Howe Sloan
Mrs. Anita Stallworth
Dr. and Mrs. Wm. S. Stoney, Jr.
Mr. William Towler
Dr. Greer Ricketson
Vanderbilt University
    Engineering School
Mr. & Mrs. Robt. Warner, Jr.
Mr. & Mrs. George W. Weesner
Mrs. Marie S. Woolwine

Friends ($100 to $499)

Mr. & Mrs. William Akers
Mr. Buck Allison, Inc.
Mrs. Sarah Ambrose

Mr. and Mrs. Michael and Heather Argo
Mrs. Paul Banks
Mr. & Mrs. Daniel B. Barge, Jr.

Dr. & Mrs. Allan D. Bass

Mrs. Frances Tisdale Bayer

Beefeater Foundation
  Rendigs Fels

Dr. & Mrs. Otto Billig

Dr. & Mrs. Eugene L. Bishop

Mr. & Mrs. John Boone

Mr. Howard Boorman

Mr. and Mrs. Reber Boult

Mr. & Mrs. Henry Brackin, Jr.

Chancellor Emeritus
  Harvie Branscomb

Bridgestone Tire
  Mr. Ishikure Kazuo

Mrs. Dorothy M. Brittingham

Harry and Marion Broquist

Mr. & Mrs. Martin Brown

Mrs. Ruthelia Buchi

Mr. & Mrs. Daniel Burton, Jr.
  Washington, D.C.

Kristina Burton
  Washington, D.C.

Mr. & Mrs. Michael Burton
  San Antonio, TX

Matthew Burton
  San Antonio, TX

Flavia Burton

Fletcher Burton
  Princeton, NJ

Dr. and Mrs. Richard Cannon

Mrs. Clarence G. Carney

Centennial Club

Dr. & Mrs. Cully A. Cobb

Mr. & Mrs. Alan G. Cohen

Dr. & Mrs. Robert D. Collins

Dr. & Mrs. Fred Cowden

Howard and Themis Poulos Cramer
  Atlanta, GA

Mrs. A. D. Creighton

Mr. John F. Cummins

Mrs. Betty Sams Daniel
  Decatur, GA

Dr. & Mrs. William J. Darby
  Thompson Station, TN

Mrs. Lipscomb Davis

Dr. Thomas and Jane Davis

Jean M. Demos
  Kifissia, Greece

Mr. John H. DeWitt, Jr.

Mr. & Mrs. W. Joe Diehl, Jr.

Mr. & Mrs. James K. Don

Mr. & Mrs. Starkey Duncan

Mr. and Mrs. Ed Dunn

Mr. & Mrs. Walter Durham

Endowment Fund of the
  Jewish Federation of
  Nashville and Middle Tennessee

Mr. Joseph Erwin, Jr.

Mrs. Annette Eskind

Dr. & Mrs. E. William Ewers

Mrs. Beatrice C. Fels

James and Toni Fogelsong

Dr. & Mrs. Richard France
  Williamsburg, VA

Mrs. Margit Friedrich
  Washington, D.C.

Dr. and Mrs. Fred Goldner

Tom and Joan Griscom, Jr.

Dr. & Mrs. Lawrence A. Grossman

H.G. Hill Co.

Dr. & Mrs. John Hammon, Jr.

Dr. & Mrs. William Hartmann

Mrs. Ann S. Hill
Wendell and Virginia Holladay
Sylvia Hyman
Chancellor Emeritus and
    Mrs. Alexander Heard
Hellenic Study Group of Atlanta
Mrs. May Buntin Hill
Mrs. Robijn Hill
Mrs. Cecelia C. Hilton
Dr. & Mrs. George W. Holcomb
Dr. and Mrs. Thomas Hudson
Mrs. Alice Ingram Hooker
Mr. & Mrs. Carl H. Hudson
Dr. & Mrs. Thomas Hudson
Mr. & Mrs. Charles A. Howell III
International Study Group
Mr. & Mrs. Clay Jackson
Mrs. Elizabeth Jacobs
Mr. & Mrs. Leland R. Johnson
Jones Mold Co.
Dr. & Mrs. R. H. Kampmeier
Herschel and Louise Katzman
Katzman/Werthan Gallery
Mr. Sidney F. Keeble, Jr.
Mrs. John Kenst
    Maryville, TN
Kiwanis Club of Nashville
Mrs. Gus D. Kuhn
Mr. & Mrs. William I. Kuhn
Mrs. Elizabeth Langford
Mr. & Mrs. Rollin Lasseter
    South Bend, IN
Mr. & Mrs. Samuel Loventhal
Mr. and Mrs. Howard P. Lucas
Miss Anne W. Magruder

Mr. Myles Maillie
Mr. & Mrs. Robt. C. Mathews
Mr. Joseph L. May
Mr. Leon May
Juanita R. McClanahan
Mr. and Mrs. E.R. McMillin
Mr. & Mrs. Robert A. McGaw
E. R. McMillan
McQuiddy Printing Co.
Ms. Sarah Moench
Mr. and Mrs. William Lynn Moench
Mr. & Mrs. Walt. Morgan, Jr.
Nashville Gas Co.
    Mr. J. William Denny
Nashville Sounds Baseball Club
J. Donald & Elizabeth Nichols
Dr. & Mrs. John Oates, Jr.
Mr. & Mrs. Robert C. Odle
Mr. and Mrs. William B. Owens
    Atlanta, GA
Carter and Linda Philips
George and Paula Pierce
Dr. Harry Lee Page
Dr. & Mrs. Takis Patikas
Jerome Pollitt
    Woodbridge, CT
Dr. & Mrs. Robert W. Quinn
Rabold and Hoover Brokerage Co., Inc.
Stanley & Jeanette Rabold
Mrs. Celeste Casey Reed
Mr. and Mrs. James E. Richards
Mr. & Mrs. John F. Richardson
Natalie J. Riven
Phillip Robinson
Mrs. Louis Rosenfeld

Patti Steebe Satler
Tish Hooker Schermerhorn
Dr. & Mrs. Stephen Schillig, Jr.
Mrs. John Shapiro
Mrs. Walter Sharp
Herbert and May Shayne
Sisk Printing Services, Inc.
Mr. & Mrs. Lester H. Smith, Jr.
Mr. & Mrs. Madison Smith
Margaret Thompson Smith
Steiner-Liff Industries
    Noah Liff
Raeburn and Carol Stiles
Mr. & Mrs. Billy T. Sumner
Earl Swensson Associates

Dr. & Mrs. John Tanner
Dr. Spencer Thornton
Dr. & Mrs. William Wadlington
Raymond and Carleen Waller
Ann B. Walling, honoring
    Mr. & Mrs. Reber Boult
Warren Co. Hist'l Society
Dr. & Mrs. Horace E. Watson
Mr. & Mrs. Albert Werthan
Bernard & Betty Werthan
Leah Rose Werthan
Mr. John Wright
Robert K. Zelle
Mr. Benjamin Zucker

Fans (to $99)

Dr. Virginia Abernethy
Mrs. Grace T. Abramchik
Mr. and Mrs. James D. Alderman
Clare Allen
Mary Allen
Dr. & Mrs. Edwin Anderson
Mr. & Mrs. George J. Anderson
Mrs. A. J. Baird
Betty Baird
Mr. and Mrs. Sam Barefield
Mr. S. Steven Barefield
Mr. & Mrs. Charles Baryames
    Lansing, MI
Mrs. E. M. Bass
Mrs. J. Alonzo Bates
    Centerville, TN
Leonard and Cicely Beach

Mr. & Mrs. Earl Beasley
Mrs. Margaret Wyatt Beasley
Mr. & Mrs. Fred Becker
Mr. & Mrs. Beezley
    Hurtsboro, AL
Anne D. Belfort
Mary C. Bell
    New York, NY
Kerstin Bergmann
    Teanick, NY
Preston N. Bissinger
Bradford Foundation
Mrs. Eleanor Bradford
Lillian R. Bradford
Dr. & Mrs. Hearn Bradley
Frank and Gina Brazil
Loyd and Linda Brewer

Harry and Marion Broquist
Terry and Peggy Burkhalter
Mr. & Mrs. Ralph Brunson
Emily C. Byrn
Mrs. Rachelle Buchanan
Mrs. Horatio B. Buntin
Calvary United Methodist Church
    The Tower Class
Julia and William Campbell
    Atlanta, GA
Mr. Thomas D. Canakes
    Dallas, TX
Robert and Harriet Cates
Mr. Nick C. Chiotras
    Berkeley, CA
Calvary United Meth. Church
Ms. Lin Church-Sitter
Dr. Virginia Clodfelter
Ben and Barbara Cobb
W. Ovid Collins, Jr.
Mr. & Mrs. Raymond Conatser
Ms. Kathryn Constantinides
    Charlotte, NC
Robert and Janet Daniel
    Homewood, AL
Mrs. J. Paschall Davis
William J. Davis
    Murfreesboro, TN
Mr. & Mrs. Ward DeWitt, Jr.
Mr. & Mrs. William J. Dickson
Mrs. Martha D. Donnelly
Mr. & Mrs. Robert B. Drews
Dr. Ted and Kathe Eastburn
Dr. Michael H. Ebert
Mr. Leon Economy
    Atlanta, GA

Mr. Christos E. Euthimiou
    Chicago, IL
Dr. J. N. Exton
Ms. Beatrice G. Fadil
    Clifton, NJ
Clara S. Fink
Marguerite and Edward A. Fish
Dr. & Mrs. Howard Foreman
Mr. & Mrs. Anthony A. Fox
    Bay Village, OH
Leo and Mary Frangis
Mr. Jack Freeman
James and Marie Fuqua
Lawrence and Helaine Fuldauer
Mr. & Mrs. John Gauld
Mr. Anthony J. George
    Gallatin, TN
Mr. & Mrs. Gus A. Georges
    St. Louis, MO
Mrs. Nicholas Georgescu-Roegen
Mrs. McPheeters Glasgow, Jr.
Golf Club Lane Gardeners
Mr. William M. Goldman
Graham Meeting Services
    and Convention Consultants
    Betty Baird Graham
Clifton & Elizabeth Greer, Jr.
Mrs. Margaret C. Groos
John and Anne Hailey
    Deerfield Beach, FL
Evelyn B. Hammond
Prf. & Mrs. Hamilton Hazlehurst, Jr.
Mrs. Robert Helton
Mrs. Harold Herman
David and Andrea Hildebrand
Henry H. Hill

Mr. Max Hiller
Mrs. Cecelia Hilton
David and Elizabeth Hoover
Centerville, TN
Mr. Henry Hopton
Horrell Properties, Inc.
Mr. E. Edward Houk
Mrs. Barbara S. Hull
Decatur, GA
Ms. Effie K. Hume
Hendersonville, TN
Carlene L. Hunt, Inc.
Ann Hutton
Mr. & Mrs. Maurice Johnson
Mr. Mike Jackson
Ms. Shelia Jackson
Dr. Rebecca H. Jacobsen
Thomson, GA
Mr. Thomas P. Kapantais
Huntington, VA
Katzman/Werthan Gallery
in honor of Louise LeQuire
Mrs. Audrey B. Kennedy
Mrs. Agnes Kezios
Atlanta, GA
Dr. & Mrs. Stothe Kezios
Atlanta, GA
Dr. & Mrs. Jerome Klein
Anne T. Knauff
Brookfield, WI
Ms. Dorothea Koukotas
Mercerville, NJ
Leontine Kubit
Mr. & Mrs. John Lachs
Mrs. Vaden Lackey, Jr.
Ms. Ruth G. Lane

Mr. & Mrs. A. R. Lansing
Magnolia, MS
Ms. Sharon Laudermilk
Goodlettsville, TN
Mrs. Catherine D. Leibovitz
Mr. John Lemondes
Liverpool, NY
Ned Lentz
Nancy L. LeQuire
Alma Lightfoot
Ronald S. Ligon
Franklin, TN
Mrs. Wister H. Ligon
Ms. Martha J. Lindsey
Leontine Fort Linton
Claude and Norma Lowe
Amy J. Martin
Robin D. Mattison
Mr. & Mrs. Carl Mays
Louise H. McCoy
Prudence McGuire
Meeting Services and
Convention Consultants
Alice C. Merritt
Dr. Kryiakos Michaelides
Atlanta, GA
Mrs. J. K. Miles
Mrs. Eula P. Miller
William H. Moenning, Jr.
Mr. & Mrs. David H. Moore
Eleanor Morrissey
D. E. Motlow
David & Cathy Mullendore
Mr. & Mrs. Charles Nelson
Ms. Rubye Evans Oritz
Orr/Hauk Associates

Ms. Adelaide B. Owens
Atlanta, GA

Ms. Nona E. Owensby
Hermitage, TN

Harry Lee Page

Mr. & Mrs. Anthony Panchares
Fort Worth, TX

Dr. Charles and Jane Park

Mrs. Margaret P. Partee

Mr. & Mrs. Angelo Paspalas
St. Louis, MO

Ms. Elizabeth H. Patch
Clarksville, TN

Ms. Rubye Patch
Clarksville, TN

Rebecca A. Patrick
Stevenson, MD

Peggy O'Neal Peden

Dr. & Mrs. Gordon Peerman
in memory of Gladys Hamilton

Billie E. Person and Carrol Miller

Mrs. Irene J. Phelps
Maineville, OH

Eleanor E. Phillips

Ernest & Patricia Pinson
Jackson, TN

P.O.E. Chapter E

Ms. Helen Polychronis
Long Island City, NY

Mr. Walter Pope

Mrs. Robert A. Porter, Jr.

Mr. Steven W. Posch

Mr. Aristides G. Poulos
Stone Mountain, GA

Mr. & Mrs. Louis J. Purcell
Mt. Juliet, TN

Joseph and Patricia Reed

Mr. & Mrs. James E. Richards

Jan B. Riven

Phillip & Christy Robinson
Madison, TN

Dr. & Mrs. Kenneth Rutherford

Mrs. Helen B. Rothermel

Patti Steebe Sattler

William & May M. Sawyer

Patricia L. Schirmer

Mr. William J. Sensing

Dr. & Mrs. Vernon Sharp

Ms. Velda Shore

Mrs. Lisa Silver

Mrs. Angelea F. Smith

Mrs. Henry Carroll Smith

Mr. David Richie Smith

Mr. Gardner O. Smith

Dr. & Mrs. Anderson Spickard

Ms. Patricia Strain

Ms. Elana M. Stuart

George and Sylvia Sullivan

United Service

Ms. Martha W. Teschan

Mr. Joe Thompson, Jr.

Mrs. Palmer Thompson

Dr. & Mrs. John N. Tiliacos
Marietta, GA

Mrs. Louise S. Tomlin

Mr. & Mrs. Stephen Trautman

Mrs. Jean VanVolkenburgh

Mr. Edward Van Voorhees

Mr. John Vasilakos
Bethpage, NY

Mrs. John A. Waites

Mr. Kenneth S. Watkins
   Childersburg, AL
Anne Beach Was
Mrs. Carol Wattleworth
Mr. & Mrs. Watzulik
Mr. & Mrs. James Weatherspoon
Mrs. Blanche H. Weaver
Eleanor Webb
Mr. and Mrs. Herbert Weismeyer

Mrs. Marilyn Whiteman
David W. and Margaret H. Wiley
Ms. Ann Scott Wilkinson
   Stone Mountain, GA
Irene Jackson Wills
Ridley Wills II
Dr. Lawrence Wolfe
Mr. and Mrs. Apostolos D. Ziros
   Marietta, GA

Official Assistants, 1982-1988

Anice Doak, 1983
Mary Mark Munday, 1984-85
James Legg, 1984
Jo Fassnacht, 1984-85
Stephane Clion, 1986
(France)
Inka Wolter, 1987
(Germany)
Colin Kohnhorst, 1987
Hisashi "Kyu" Yamamoto, 1988-90
(Japan)

Volunteer Assistants, 1982-1988

Andree Akers
Will Akers
Chris Armstrong
Terry Arthur
Martha Berry
Victoria Boone
Tim Cambell
Luisa D'Artista
Jack Dews

Susan Bostick Fassnacht
Annie Freeman
Stanley Friedman
Sydelle Friedman
Sherbe Frank Green
Klaus Hansen
Katrina Hoem
(Norway)
Robijn Hill

Socrates Ioannides

Bill Jackson

Linda Jones

Vaden Lackey

Cloe Lenderman

Louise LeQuire

David Lockyear

Mark Van Loon

Myles Maillie

Juanita McClanahan

Debbie McCroskey

Joyce McCroskey

Elizabeth McGaw

Carol Mitchell

Leila Montegue

Michael Page

Betty Partee

Thomas Pennington

Nancy Roche

Anne Roos

Jim Sherraden

Patti Tauscher

Cati Vietoriscz

Judy Wolgast

BIBLIOGRAPHY

THE PARTHENON:

Alberts, Robert C., *Benjamin West: A Biography* (Boston 1978)

Baigell, Matthew, *Dictionary of American Art* (New York 1979)

Bruno, V. (ed.), *The Parthenon* (New York 1974)

Economakis, Richard, ed., *Acropolis Restoration: The CCAM Interventions* (London 1994)

Egerton, John, *Nashville: The Face of Two Centuries* (Nashville 1979)

Herington, C.J., *Athena Parthenos and Athena Pallas* (Manchester 1955)

Hooker, G.T.W. (ed.), *Parthenos and Parthenon* (supplement X to *Greece and Rome*) (Oxford 1963)

Jenkins, Ian, *The Parthenon Frieze* (London 1994)

Johnson, Leland, *The Parks of Nashville.* (Nashville, 1986).

Justi, Herman, ed., *Official History of the Tennessee Centennial Exposition* (Nashville 1898)

Kelly, Franklin, *Frederic Edwin Church* (Washington, D.C. 1989)

Korres, Manolis, *From Pentelicon to the Parthenon* (Athens, Greece 1995)

Mansfield, J.M., *The Robe of Ahena and the Panathenic Peplos*, (Ph.D. Dissertation, University of California at Berkeley, 1985)

Moulder, George B., *The Parthenon at Nashville*, (Nashville 1931)

Pansanias, *Guide to Greece* (Hammondsworth 1971)

Plutarch, *Life of Pericles* (Hammondsworth 1971)

Pollitt, J.J., *Art and Experience in Classical Greece* (Cambridge 1972)

Thuss, W. G. and A. J., *Art Album of the Tennessee Centennial and International Exposition* (Nashville 1975)

Tournikiotis, Panayotis, ed., *The Parthenon and Its Impact in Modern Times* (Athens, Greece 1994)

Waller, William, ed. *Nashville in the 1890s* (Nashville 1970)

Wilson, Benjamin Frank III, *The Parthenon of Periclese and its Reproduction in America*, (Nashville, 1937)

Woodford, Susan, *The Parthenon* (Cambridge 1981)

ANCIENT SCULPTURE:

Ashmole, B., *Architect and Sculptor in Classical Greece* (New York 1972)

Boardman, J. and D. Finn, *The Parthenon and Its Sculptures* (Austin 1985)

Boardman, J., *Greek Sculpture: The Classical Period* (London 1985)

Browning, Robert, ed., *The Greeks: Classical, Byzantine and Modern* (New York 1985)

Cook, B.F., *The Elgin Marbles* (London 1984)

Fine, John, *The Ancient Greeks: A Critical History* (Cambridge 1983)

Green, Peter, *Ancient Greeks: An Illustrated History* (London 1973)

Harrison, E.B., "The Composition of the Amazonomachy on the Shield of Athena Parthenos." *Hesperia* 35 (1966) pp.107-133.

Kagan, Donald, *Pericles of Athens and the Birth of Democracy: The Triumph of Vision in Leadership* (New York 1991)

Leipen, N., *Athena Parthenos: a Reconstruction* (Toronto 1971)

Levi, Peter, *Atlas of the Greek World* (New York 1980)

Read, H., "The Monument and the Amulet" in *The Art of Sculpture* (Princeton 1977) pp.3-24.

Ridgway, B.S., *Fifth Century Styles in Greek Sculpture* (Princeton 1981)

Robertson, M. and A. Frantz, *The Parthenon Frieze* (New York 1975)

Smith, A.H., *The Sculptures of the Parthenon*, (London, 1910)

Wilshire, Susan Ford, *Greece, Rome and the Bill of Rights* (Norman, Oklahoma 1992)

ARCHITECTURE:

Artman, John H., and Kropa, Susan, *Ancient Greece Independent Learning Unit* (Pasippary, New Jersey 1991)

Coulton, J.J., *Ancient Greek Architects at Work* (Ithaca 1977)

Dinsmoor, W.B., *The Architecture of Ancient Greece* (New York 1975)

Lawrence, A.W. (rev. R.A. Tomlinson), *Greek Architecture* (Hammondsworth 1983)

Palagia, Olga, *The Pediments of the Parthenon* (Leiden, The Netherlands 1993)

Penrose, F.C., *The Principles of Athenian Architecture*, (London 1851)

Tomlinson, R.A., *Greek Sanctuaries* (New York 1976)

DORIC ORDER

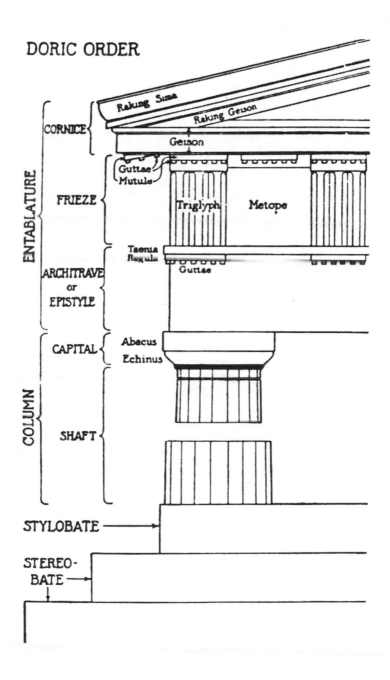

Raking Sima

Raking Geison

Geison

CORNICE

Guttae
Mutule

Triglyph   Metope

FRIEZE

Taenia
Regula

Guttae

ARCHITRAVE
or
EPISTYLE

ENTABLATURE

Abacus
Echinus

CAPITAL

COLUMN

SHAFT

STYLOBATE ⟶

STEREO-
BATE ⟶

That Which is Round Can Be No Rounder

Women's Work

"Whatever may be necessary to preserve the sanctity of the home and ensure the freedom of the same"
— Kate Kirkman

This monument was erected on the site of the Women's Building at the Tennessee Centennial Exposition in 1897 by the Centennial Club after the buildings had been removed. The members were: Mrs. John W. Thomas, Miss Mary B. Temple, Mrs. Florence K. Droullard, Mrs. Charles N. Grosvenor, Mrs. Robert Weakley, Miss Ada Scott Rice.